I am Soulpoet: 18 Years of Vision in Verse

NILS ODHNER

⊥L

Aditsan Press
Chicago
2015

DEDICATION

I dedicate this book to life itself. To quote the Dead, what a "long, strange trip it's been." Indeed!

CONTENTS

ACKNOWLEDGMENTS

I am indebted to…

God, who has stood with me and carried my aching bones and feeble soul all the times I couldn't carry myself;

My mother, Carroll Odhner, who has nurtured my love for literature with her quiet, gentle love and encouragement;

Audris Rozelle Odhner, my wife and the love of my life, and Skye Marion-Jane Odhner, my precious daughter, because of whom my light shines so brightly;

Friends and family, near and far: for being patient and walking with me as I blazed all those unexpected, long and winding trails to get here;

My dear writer friends from Elcy's: each of you has a deep, familiar place in my heart. You have helped me to become the poet and man that I am by sharing your lives with me in words;

Everyone from my spiritual circles – from the New Church to Calvary to Trinity, and all recovering folks in the rooms: without you helping me get sober and grow spiritually I would cease to thrive and my words would be empty metaphors;

I am a blessed man for all of your unconditional love and support over the years.

Yours in Love and Devotion,
Nils

IN THE POET'S OWN WORDS

I Am Soulpoet: 18 Years of Vision in Verse paints a verbal portrait of my life experience.

Writing, and poetry in particular, expresses my keenest method of interacting with this often paradoxical and painful world.

The journey started on a balmy night in March of 1995, a few months after I had left my parents' home with nothing more than a pack of Marlboro reds and the shirt on my back.

I was living at a "hippie house" that was a magnet for lost souls. Drugs and idealistic jargon were the norm, as well as addiction, depravity, and chaos.

Little did I know, that warm March night – the same night of the Grateful Dead's last tour in Philadelphia – would turn into the beginning of a lifetime soul journey, as I tripped my brains out, seeing colors, pondering concepts, and feeling things I did not think humanly possible.

That first acid trip bust my psychic channel open just enough to enable me to begin expressing these insights in words, less than a month after my parents had whisked me away to my brother's house in rural Pennsylvania.

On April 9, 1995, I sat alone, barbecuing a piece of fish. This became the subject of my first poem. Thereafter, I began to think in terms of describing what I saw, everywhere, and what I thought and felt, and put it on paper at every opportunity.

The rest, as they say, is history.

Please partake of my most lucid and brutally real visions, captured in verse.

NILS ODHNER

ON WRITING

All These Things for Which I Write

I want to tell you all
About all my excitements and joys
Every emotion, every appreciation,
Everything I taste, every great song,
Everything that triggers heaven in my soul

I want to tell you all
All that and more
And that is why I write
That's why I'm a poet
A stupid fool but words won't show it
But everything I love and loathe
And philander and fear
And immense joys and sorrows
Enlivenments and contrivances,
Joyfulness and annoyances—
Everything under the sun,
The moon, the stars, the solar system,
In your soul, in those dark spaces
Inside the earth and within
Undiscovered realms of birth and light—
It is all these things for which I write.

I want to tell you all
About all my everything that ends up
Here, on paper.
Why? Because it saves my soul,
MY LIFE, gives this existence meaning.
Play some jazz and give me
A tub of Ben and Jerry's and
I don't need no promised life of heaven—
I just want to tell you what is heaven to me,
About everything that's free,
About everything that makes this life
Rock like the world's happiest par-tee.

I want to tell you all
All that and more
And that is why I write
That's why I'm a poet

A stupid fool but words won't show it
But everything I have experienced in my life,
Everything I have experienced on this very night—

It is all these things for which I write.

Security Columnist

I feel good today
Seeing my name and words
In print in a real magazine
And I write about security
And security strategies
I am now told
I'm an informed source
Yet
I don't really know much about security
Perhaps I'll learn as I go
It's like life
It's like me relating to you
I really know nothing about security
Except that by writing this
And trying to practice what I write
I may be a strong arm of security
For you
Little secret: I'm really insecure
But try ways and paths I don't know at all
And thereby find strength
And by association, security
I want you to be able to feel safe around me
Though I know little of security
I want you to trust that this is a
Trusted environment
Even though humans, like servers,
Fail from time to time
I want your real signature,
The one on your heart
To reside within my firewall
I want this, yes, I want you all
To see that I know little of security
Yet we are all here at the same ball
Learning to shape our intuitions
And our hearts and minds to what is safe
For you, for me, and for us all.

My Journal (My Ticket)

This journal is where I toss my scrawl.
Its pages are where I lay down,
With aplomb, all I've thought,
And heard, and did, and saw.

This journal is where my fingers ache
My bleeding heart,
Where I bring my chains of torment,
My hopes, my dreams,
And joys, and call it art.

This is my journal
And it's where I piss and moan.
It's the fertile, moist and gentle ground
Upon which seeds are sown.

Seeds:
Of hope,
Of full disclosure,
Of mending fences and rebuilding bridges,
Of tossing my cares to the winds of change,
Of letting go and letting God,
Of moving past the evil things I've thought and done,
Of acceptance,
Of sobriety,
Of charity,
Of helping others,
And most of all,
Of Love.

My journal is the seedbed
Of such wonders, the grove
For saplings to become trees
That will one day stand up to
Thunder, driving rain, winds,
And fierce strokes of lightning.

Meanwhile, these trees will be fighting:
Weathering the storms, growing thicker bark,
Roots going deep and broad,

Deep and broad, until they scar the earth's surface
And tear away the sod.

My journal gives birth to such strength.
I am merely a man -
Broken,
Powerless,
Perverse,
Arrogant,
Misanthropic,
Desperate,
Conniving,
Angry,
Lost,
Foolish.
My journal enables me to sketch
These attributes in elocutions
And images and riddles,
And in so doing turn my thoughts
To God, and Light, and Love
And being whole again.

My journal is the most intimate place
I'll ever know,
And the most nestled, cozy cave
I'll ever rest my bones.

My journal gives these rotten,
Dry bones life
When to stay inside my head
Is a curse worse than death.

My journal is a conduit, a conductor
Of the Divine.
My journal is my safety valve,
My medicine,
That allows my light to shine.

My journal is mine.
My journal is me,
My journal is my ticket out.
My journal sets me free.

18 Years

18 years, almost to the day:
April 9, 1995.

That first poem
Came gushing out of me
Raw like sewage
From the contaminated pits
Of a bitter cesspool.

Rebellion and futility
Dogged my every step
And thought,
Step and thought,
Step and thought...

18 years
Of drunken, drugged
Escapades,
Of nights wondering why
We were all made,
When I looked up
At the moon and stars,
And vast canopy of black sky.

18 years chiseling rough stones
So recklessly till my fingers bled,
Along with my soul...
Into elocuted statues and figurines
That showed me:

Death
Life
Fear
Beauty
Pain
Nature
Hope
Horror
Love
Ugliness

Oblivion
Obsession
Compulsion
Utter desolation
Utter depravity
Mental Anguish
Emotional Fits
Triumph
Faith
Evil
The Devil
God
Torture
Serenity
Eternity
Mental Fortitude

All these experiences, attributes, states,
And more were carved and sweated
Onto pages and pages
Keystrokes on a computer
In a manic frenzy...

18 years,
Almost to the day:
Several articles,
A few short stories and poems,
And a book published.
A degree in Writing and English.

Now these 18 years
Serve a new purpose -
To teach,
To collaborate,
To mentor,
To achieve my dreams
As a writer
Along with my dear friends
Who are on the same path.

Miracles do happen -
But not without:

The love,
The daily dues,
The training / education
(formal or otherwise),
And most of all -
Insane passion and persistence!

18 years of writing is now
Graduating to the next level :).

REAL LOVE

Let Me Sauté Your Feast

Pass the Olive Oil, Garlic and Ginger
Please,
Just sit back and let me sauté your feast.

I want to cook for you,
Salmon that melts in your mouth,
Steamed organic peas, sweet potatoes—

Please just sit back and
Let me cook for you
I want to cook for you
And feed your senses to Nirvana
I have to cook for you,
It's the only thing I wanna
Do until the sky turns black to blue
And stars fall from the heavens
And all the slot machines
Turn to lucky sevens.

I want to feed your soul
With food, BBQ Chicken Extraordinaire
Chocolate-covered strawberries,
Butter, cholesterol on a piece of homemade bread.

I want to cook for you
Let me cook for you
I want you to bite each bite
To climactic bliss and ecstasy
And feel so soft and whisper things

Like, "that was better than the best I've ever had."
"Every time you cook I feel so glad, so glad, so glad."

So I will cook for you
On whatever occasion you want me to
Just pass the Olive Oil, Garlic, and Ginger
Please,
And let me sauté your feast.

Wordless Knowing

I do not need
Your love or acceptance
To sustain me.

I prefer to bask
In my "ruling love":
Getting blissed out
Through poetry
And the music that it brings.

I am content
And peaceful
And I love
Who I have become.

I do not need
The love or affection
Of another
To fill
What is already filled.

But, if you meet me
In that sacred, equal place,
I will be happy
To dance with you,
To smile while you smile,
And speak silence,
A wordless knowing,
That were are THERE.

Your Intuition

It was your intuition
Not mine
That saw something
Heard something
Smelled something
Felt something
Perceived something

I did nothing
Except
Follow my bliss
Put my past behind me
Learn to love others
Learn to listen
Learn to just be
And thereby
Find the peace of God
And the true joy
Of loving
Every day

I just showed up
On your proverbial doorstep
But didn't realize the fact
It was like magic
It is synchronicity
Everything aligned
Divine timing

But it was your intuition
That led the way
And all I had to do
Was get out of the way

I like how things
Good things
Just flow
Without restraint
That is how it is
So I will take this ride

That your intuition
Long ago decided
Was the right one

Cultivation

My soul is transparent before you.
You perceive my heart
Beneath translucent skin.
As with God,
There is nothing I can hide from you.
Nor is there
Anything I would want to hide from you.

I am an open book
And you can read me.
Every special thought or notion,
You can see it.
Every breath that blows
In and out,
You can breathe it.

And – I you.

Our visions, our hearts,
Our talents, our faiths,
Are aligned.
One – Heart, Thought, Action –
Devotion
Emotion
Oceans and new shores
Call us:
The majesty of beloved earth
And nurturing souls
Through writing and art
And
Cultivating the soil
Cultivating gardens of growth
Growth of the Spirit.

Being fed with good things,
My heart rings.
I no longer ask,
"How could it be?"
For it is –
The beginning of a lifetime journey.

EARTH & SKY

The Clouds (What Are They Really?)

How many leaves might there be?
How many grains of sand by the sea?
Infinity, infinity, if that will suffice.
The clouds, the clouds, what are they really?
Animals, animals, all shapes and kinds.
Which one captures your essence divine?
Fearsome protector, defender, Mama Lion;
Yet wise and perceptive, loving and kind.
A dolphin, a dolphin—such of like mind.
All of these beings, reflections in the sky,
Become the ocean in their due course of time.

The Rocks

What holiness enshrined –
That roll, amass in time;
That stand and oversee
Every feather, every tree,

And know in ages past
The ices and their wrath.
Behold with awe, they stand:
Long before the hand of man.

Sunset Triptych

SUNSET I: EARTHLING FULLNESS

Was it ever different?
Was this all before?
Shadowed red & purple black,
The earthling fullness gives it back.

Deflected rays amaze and tease;
Starling sings, "there exists a Deity!"
Spackled onward, what Thou art—
Will the stillness ever frown?

SUNSET II: GRAND DIVINING STEW

With much affright
I stare into this tapestry,
The wind about me cool & soft,
The night is raising, ever-praising,
All the light in climbing spheres.

We set the white & yellow cloud
From charcoals that mix the hue
Into the grand divining stew.

SUNSET III: THE SILENT HUE

My sanctuary as I stare into the blue
Hides nothing, no frown nor dampened wind—
You see me sit there now & then,
Uplifted, skyward, silent, not a hint
Of sadness, anger, melancholy:

POURING GOLDNESS hides
--the shadow--,
Brings upon, unleashed into my eyes--:

Ageless wonder, the masque of decadence,
The birth of dawning structures

Sprung from chaos ceasing, the empty
Something that the sky declares;

The empty something, silent calling,
Newness falling from the spectrum of the sun—

Shields in clouds and faces streaming,
Comedy of the journey we are taking,

Endless stream of white and bitter
Tamed into what I call the silent hue—

The Burdocks

If you think about what the
Grove of 10-foot tall burdocks
Are to ants, it makes the
Skyscrapers of New York
Wan in comparison.
These natural monoliths
Are greater than anything made
By the hands of man,
From the Bean Trees
Under which we sit
Writing thoughts like these,
To the Redwoods and Sequoias
Out West, which exist
Like myths of dreams
We have yet to see.

Cataract Lake Poem

Sitting on a fallen log
Over a rushing stream
Near Cataract Lake,
One is amazed by the
Pure meditation of sound,
Sunlight scintillating off
The water and brown rocks,
And the pristine divinity of
The towering hemlocks
That climb the mountainside.
On the grassy knolls and
Rolling hills, light green
Mountain shrubs lead the way
To the goldening Aspens,
Stately even when
Carved in by human hands.
And then there's the lake itself,
Peaceful and blue, reflecting
The yellows of the Aspens,
And the green-blue of the
Colorado Blue Spruce high above.
And anchoring all of these
Revelata of the Grand Spirit of Earth
Are the Rock Faces, which
Seldom change with time
And the insignificant hands of man.
Oh, what ecstasy it is
To call this place home,
With one day in these saintly
mountains
Before returning to the hub-bub
Of civilization.

The Isle of Skye

The tide is low on the Isle of Skye;
The sun is shining, and spirits are high.

On yonder hills of heather and sheep,
A poet stamps and muddies his ancestral feet.

Ljungberg: The Heather Mountain,
The stream running crystalline, as a fountain.

Eons ago, the Swedes, the Vikings,
Invaded, and took this land to their liking.

It is ancient, it is volcanic, it is shamanic,
For the spirit calls him back, runic, talismanic, (to)

The stones and crevices on the Isle of Skye,
Where the sun is shining, and spirits are high.

Purple mountains majesty is no compare
To this beyond Ice Age land so fair.

The poet bends his head, takes it in,
Becomes the Isle where land, water, and sky begin.

(Missing Verses):

*He thinks: "I will name my daughter Skye,
After this great Isle, where seagulls cry."*

*Of course, motherly approval for this name
Is pending, for then and only then,
Could this tale have a perfect ending!*

Early Spring Rain

The essence of love is:
The early spring rain,
Pushed forth from
Directions unknown,
Intermittent as it sweeps
Across the landscape
In a windy fury,
Its pulse, its center,
Its heartbeat undetectable.

The early spring rain
Strikes its observer
With a damp encasement
That cuts past the sinews,
Through the viscera,
And lodges in the bones.

The early spring rain
Nourishes the slowly waking
Womb of Mother Earth.
Seedlings lodged beneath
Her surface are given
A vital flow that will erupt
In new flora as the sun
Waxes closer to its fullness,
Day by day.

The early spring rain covers
All but a barren countryside.
Like the human being
Standing in its path,
What matures and grows
To the glory of fruition
In due time
Is hidden
For but a fleeting moment
In the rolling consciousness
Of time.

MUSINGS

Social

Too bad your way of being social
Ain't my way of being social;

To you it takes a man of letters
Someone who can do it better
Than my way of doing things.

For me to read a book is social,
To know your name and date of birth is social;
To scope the scene with horn-rimmed glasses
And to wear these clothes so grey and clashing,
To find a way to make you laugh
And put myself out on a limb is being social.

I may not have the looks to kill,
To fit your book of being social;
I may not use those words of skill
Which in my world could bring us closer.

Why not lay in bed and dream the social,
Or sit in darkened corner 'till the cows come home?

Why all this bump and grind for social,
Why the perfect legs and perfect mass?

* * *

To pretend I'm yours I'll drink the social,
To know the ways of mind I'll trip the social,
Try a thousand times, I'll never move
'Em shakers the way that you do.

Who's to say my racing mind ain't social,
Dunkin' Donuts and your Denny's fries—
Social or not—they can pass the time.

* * *

But, you know those street side mimes are social,

Each and every circus freak is social,
Damn!, those Star Trek nerds are social!

Guess that makes the brute and tattooed sailor social,
Everyone who's lost a limb is social,
Even those who look like a certain animal
And act exactly in its favor are social.

So you thought I wasn't social?
Well, I gladly beg to differ,
Now that I've thought about it some.

I don't need to tell you what is superficial,
Or antisocial, or any thing that ever
Rubs you upside 'gainst the grain—

It's for you to figure what is social
And what is not.

Need the Snow Oh Oh So Bad…(Sigh)…But…I'll Have to Settle for Something Else

So the sky's about to storm…

I turn my head for just a second,
There goes the horn that is the angry gods
Unleashing howling wind.

I wish it would, I wish it could—
Perhaps just flood the day away,
Or maybe even snow at least a foot.

No Profanity

The Irish Catholic Cafeteria.
Quite a place, that reminds me of kindergarten.
And smells like piss. Well, that was only part of it.
Grown men and women. Emotionally like children.
Little sign that says 'Boys.' Little handle.
Below the waist. Yep, it smelled like piss.
And yes, it reminded me of kindergarten.
No profanity. Irish Catholics. Alcohol.
Emotionally like children.

The Sounds of Wasted Time

The sound of wasted time: tick-tock, tick-tock, tick-tock.
The incessant, anxious, repeated attempts to appear busy:
Click-click, click-click, click-click.
The ALT-Tab combo on your keyboard
And the right index finger against your mouse
Are the trigger positions for the moments
Your bosses unexpectedly hover behind you,
Glance over, perhaps peer over your shoulders.

Your head shifts back and forth
From laptop screen to large monitor
Like a printer ribbon furiously cranking out ink
On the page, an intelligent machine
Juggling emails, spreadsheets, and complex business logic.

It's all a charade, you think, your heart thrumming:
Blip-blap, blip-blap, blip-blap, within your chest.
Your brain grows foggy, your breath grows heavy,
Your eyes grown bleary.

This screen game and brain drain is killing your spirit,
All but extinguishing the sickly flame,
All that remains of your creativity.

All this time, all this wasted time, you think.
And pause and stop, and once again fire away
With your trigger hands: Alt-tab, click, Alt-tab, click,
Alt-tab, click.

You've become a senseless robot.
You used to move fluidly, thoughts in flux,
And radiate more color than Technicolor.
Now you're simply black and white,
And occasionally gray – the gray comes
When you stare at the spaces between the lines
In spreadsheets where those elusive gray dots appear.

Yeah, Facecrack!

We are all Threadheads
Addicted to Facecrack.

What began as idealism has evolved
Into self-serving lunacy.

We eat up "Likes" and "Comments"
Like they are the last morsels
In a concentration camp mess hall line.

Our heads twitch at an angle,
Checking for signs
Of the illuminating Status Indicator
On our smartphones.

We check and think Facecrack in our sleep.
We give up all desires
For that electro-frazzle peak.

We Threadheads
Are all addicted to Facecrack.
We compulsively join, route and pillage,
And get ourselves exiled
From Facebook groups of all kinds.

We are sly devils who ruin threads
By taking them over
And making them our own
Though the use of hyperbole,
Character assassination,
Or just plain stalking behavior.

In our world,
Facebook is a noun, a verb, a place,
A philosophy, a destination, a lover,
And a cruel master who calls the shots.

At work, we multitask
In between hits of Facecrack
Just to feel normal.

Our first line
With a new co-worker is:
"Facebook me."
We are the Threadheads
Addicted to Facecrack.
MySpace was just low-grade weed
Compared to this,
Our baseline chronic.

Facecrack has got us.
The children get neglected,
We say things and regret them,
We've no restraint of pen or tongue
In this warzone, jungle and home
We call Facebook.

"Unfriending" gets the best of us,
Infuriates us as though we were ripped off
By a generous dealer
Who supplied us
With a steady stream of "Likes"
And flirtatious comments in the past.

Facecrack is surreptitious
And we Threadheads can never get enough.
Yeah, Facecrack!

NIGHTTIME INTERLUDES

Into the Eternal Night

The cool solstice air whispers in soft clarity
To the light of the full moon.
Mystic searchers light candles,
Reeling their consciousness
Into the flickering, trance-inducing flame.

He picks up the guitar and sings praises
To the Goddess of the Deep,
From whence his soul emerged
Out of starlight, water, and primordial fire
Before space and time could record it.

Shivers up and down his spine
Bring the Goddess back,
Through his sweet voice,
Through E-minor to G
And then E-minor to C.

She called his name and wrote this song,
Through his voice and fingertips,
And now he plays,
Enthralled by the chilly night,
The quiet, and the flickering flame
Reflecting on the glass coffee table.

In the outside world, he is as flawed
And imbalanced as a person can be,
But in the world of the solstice moon
And its strong northerly winds on high,
He is a spirit riding the wings of the winds
Into the Eternal Night.

Thoughts on Religion

All over the world, their dots light up a dark landscape.
Each dot is glowing, pulsing with a dim light,
But left to its own devices,
That light will fade out into the darkness,
Like a distant star in the great galaxy.

Each of the billions of dim lights –
Some buzzing incessantly, some sporadically,
Like fireflies on a midsummer's night –
Seek to be reconnected, reunited with their Source,
The Love that created them each
As that tiny beam of light, so small in the big, dark world.
Their stories are older than the millennia,
And as ancient as the earth itself:
It is the story of humanity.

So the plight of the slowly fading lights,
Each a soul seeking to be reconnected and reunited,
Begs this question:
Just how, or by what means,
Shall this reconnection or reuniting take place?

The answer is thus:
Through the prophets that foretold of a Great Man,
A Savior, the One who made his Divinity Human
To dwell among us, as people.
The most important premise is this:
That we all need to reconnect,
To be reunited as humans with the Divine Source.

If you look at the word, "religion,"
It doesn't actually mean an organized structure
Prone to human fallibility and treachery.
It means, from its Latin root, "Re" + "Ligio,"
To "reunite" or "reconnect."

So the purpose of all these slowly fading lights
That dot our world is to reconnect and reunite with that Source.
Being "religious" doesn't have to mean, necessarily,
What you've been taught growing up:

That you better go to church, or else,
Or the wrath of God will smite you dead.

No, real religion is about peace
And accepting the Divinity
That many throughout this world
Have come to know, embrace, and truly live.
And the product is happiness through usefulness,
And an Eternal Life through Your Maker.

Light Healing Inner Conflict

We wear conflict not on our sleeves,
But as adorning tapestries in our inner beings.
Unanswered questions bounce to and fro,
To be lodged in some unseen crevice
Waiting to be found by the light, and we know –

Waiting and not knowing all the answers to life,
Is something special and divine.
The message from the Light is to meditate,
To circumvent our woes, to expose them;
To evolve, to embrace your being, all 360 degrees,
With loving arms of acceptance of the spiritual fight,
Of the fright from doctrines that leave you petrified.

God would not have that we live in fear.
Fear is the opposite of faith.
Light and fear cannot mutually exist –
They are exclusive of one another.
With each deep breath the conflict melts
Into the far reaches of the cosmos,
And with it light more brilliant and pristine
Than thousands of full moons combined
Saturates your being.
You are loved – by those dear to you,
By God, by life itself.

Moon Meditation

Outside, a chilly wind
Ushers swaths of gray cloud
Across the yellow, swollen moon.

An alien sheen
Bathes the night landscape
Of small yards
And shoebox-like houses.

The journeyman takes a breath,
And listens, devoid of thought,
To the interplay of echoing violin,
Flute, sitar, and sacred hums.

As the music approaches
A steadily-building climax,
His eyes blur and then focus,
Blur and then focus, focus…

…on the candle's flame
In front of him.
Sage and sweetgrass
Burn in slow fire,
Embers emitting a dense,
Balmy smoke that extracts
All negativity from this special place –
Both inside the journeyman's mind,
And heart,
And in the small shack
Where he resides.

Before time began,
Aditsan was listening.
This music was in his soul,
Germinated, encoded
In the seeds and eggs
Of his forebears,
And the Bliss
Heretofore unbeknownst
Was there as well.

Dancing Light

Behind the blinking stars,
High above, behind, within, beyond
The canopy, the fabric of pure blackness
Pierced by miniscule, dancing light –

A wizard not of human form
Pulls levers attached to ethereal strings,
Generating signals, blips of light
Asynchronously, until, as the observer
Stares in wonder at the little lights,
They form a timed, syncopated pattern,
Like a drum beat without sound.

The whites of the observer's eyes
Grow large and round, with fright,
And awe, from the moment that
She saw the intelligence register
As signals in her synapses, the lever
Clacks distinct within her mind.

From where did the intelligence
Originate? Inside the human mind,
Or from a Universal Mind, alien,
Yet familiar, and only perceptible
In nighttime interludes,
Where the cosmos defines its
Own laws and comes out to play?

MINOR-KEY VERSES

Darkened Night

Ample waves caress thy feet,
Whisper sand and glistening gloss;
Bye Bye tide the moon has set,
The seagull sings the darkened night.

Upon the pier a troubadour laments,
A ballad of the Russian Rue;
Red escapes from weakened pulse,
Cries the sky in shades of blue.

On the cliff Porphyria plays
With her prince, the pauper lad;
Down in fleece and satin lace,
Strokes the wind across her face.

In the heavens Orion waits
For the frenzied Venus, evening star;
Brighter, brighter grows the haze
Of the Milky Way in far off space.

In the sea the mermaid weeps,
Pisces, eau-trod her disgrace;
Rescinding moon bathes her back,
As the dark side hides her pale face.

Medusa slithes in swamps afar,
Stonehenge Hermes in her guard;
Beauty lies in shadow light,
Magnified by darkened night.

Lost and Crying (And Tired of Dying)

From whence comes that spark,
Which tears at the sheer density of emptiness?

What instills that sense of weightlessness,
Of faith and total lack of fear,
In this universe, in the air of this atmosphere?

Why does oblivion always become the aim,
When fusion, rather than fission,
Is what humanity's ideals seek to claim?

Idealism is dead.
Morality is an empty vault,
Robbed of precious jewels,
A freshly-dug crypt buried and to remain.

God, a Heavenly Father, a Compassionate Buddha,
An all-loving spirit, why sell this shtick?

The children lost in the wilderness
Are hungry and on the verge of dying.
The old paradigm of salvation is just one big lie,
Swallowed, hardened, and shattered by more lying,
And once ingested, innocently as candy
Into the mouths of these babes,
One can hear them crying.

Look around, ye elder statesmen,
And see the death you're turning your eyes from
And denying, while people run around sick,
Possessed, detached from their masters,
Far beyond dying.

See the crack cocaine that's sold
In magazines, and worse yet behind computer screens,
In the clothing isles, in our homes,
Behind religion's guise.
A sick culture selling sex to anyone,
Exploiting everyone, even our most young,
And hooking people without their knowing.

What about, like the Bible says,
"the voice of one crying out in the wilderness?"
'Can you feel and free my cry?'
That hurt, neglected, prisoner child sighs,
Snot and the blood of his crosses
Running from his face down to his thighs.

This crazy dream: insanity, fantasy,
Total separation from reality—
"The dream of hell" has to end, and end today.

For those of us lost and crying and tired of dying
And suffocating on all that's possessed us,
We wave our flags of surrender,
For we can fight no more.

Our Gods are dead.
Our morality is bankrupt,
Buried by bloodshed
And total hypocritical senselessness.
Our angels have deserted us.
We are hooked on this deadly culture.
You turn your heads from us,
Our cries get louder,
For we can take no more.

And now that we have died,
We dream a new dream for this planet,
For a new generation of children
To live free of the abuse—
Personally, psychically, physically—
That we have endured.

Poison Rain

A prophetic rapper said,
"A hate much greater than you could know."
Well, you know that hate much greater
Than all else, the poison that pushes
Through your pores like water through a sieve.

It's sick, man, and into your brain it quickens
Like mercury to the neurons of the mad hatter;
What a clatter, all the white noise of brain cells
And hopes destroyed and the evil of hatred employed
In its place as you race around, a vertigo spin
And darkness pins you and injects you
With its deep, dreamless tonic.

Yeah, it's more blistering than chronic smoked
From a spliff packed with rocks that make bells chime
In your head like the bells of Chartres Cathedral.
Sadly, it's the only way you know to heal,
The only pleasure sensation you can feel.
What the fuck is real?, you think before the drug hit
Slams your brain, and all the insane thoughts regress
And your blood flow quickens and you digress to a fetal curl.

Then, you're awakened rudely, hurled against a brick wall,
An empty, rank alley is your hall, your shrine,
The inverted divine where the likeness of your troubled kind
Spout off amoral rhymes and kill and fuck each other over,
And the girls, the women…Oh the women…
Not what your poor mother wanted for you,
Bloody foolish heart always screwing up your life
And leaving you abandoned in perpetual night.

So fist after fist collide against your skull,
Fingers of authorities and gangstas blurring
By your line of sight as you
Lose your life,
Lose your light,
Lose your mind,
And find your plight.

On this warm, rainy June night, as you lie dying,
Beaten in the alley, a once promising life
Given way to gunshots in the night,
Your dear mother cries herself to sleep,
Yes, weeps for your lost soul;
She prays to Jesus, the One she knows
Will free us from sin, if we only turn to Him.

But the gashes that ripped away your skin
Tore too deep, and kept bleeding, bleeding,
While the demons kept feeding
And lodging their meathooks under your bones –
And you're trapped, cut off from the light
That once shone on your gentle forehead
And soft hair, back when you really cared,
And loved and smiled and ran for miles
Into the setting sun of a future, palatable,
So much that you could taste it,
So much that you could baste it up with sauce
And cook it on the grill…
Oh that smell, of hope…
Now acquiesced to hell.

Hell…it's gelled over you, screwed you,
Imbued you, shoed you in to that life of sin.
Now tell me, please, can the Lord save a soul like him?

Dissed Grace

Disgrace.
Dis-grace.
Dissed grace.
Yeah, dissed and fallen,
According to the Callen.

Disease.
Dis-ease.
Dissed ease.
Yeah, dissed and shaken,
From black space dreams have wakened.

Dismissed.
Dis-missed.
Dissed, missed.
Yeah, dissed and missed,
Written off as one of the lost,
Only to be prayed for as a waif
That is no longer…"saved."

Dissed from:
Grace, Ease, Missed.
Grace, ease,
Yeah, Gracie's the name
Of a little girl who knows
Unconditional love.

Missed:
By many, by the beautiful, lovely,
Vagabond set.

I would rather be fallen and
Disgraced, diseased, and dismissed
By a set that can't see the world
Outside of the "lost/saved" paradigm.

I would rather be your brother,
Unconditionally,
And walk through the fire with you.

PRAYERS & MEDITATIONS

A Simple Prayer

What plan does the Creator have in mind
Each and every time the writer picks up his pen?
Even the confused, fragmented thoughts,
Sensations and feelings must mean something,
Pointing in some direction: What does it mean?
Where within the scope of hope & despair lies a prayer?

Down on my knees, pray,
One thing I'm sure that I can see...
Wearing shoes when shreds of glass appear:
That's God showing up;
Crying pain is swept away—
That's God cleansing me.
Waiting for the hourglass to pass its final grain—
That's God saying we should be
Doing something else, getting off our ass.
Ass-backwards, that's not God, not
The Man who reigns o'er the skies and clouds.

How to reach Him, how to touch Him,
How to reconnect? How to see ourselves
Through the lifeless, bloodless nightmare
In which dirt and grinding sands
Have dried up our veins?
Why be living, walking like we're dead?
You and me, we must each walk the maze,
No escaping all that's thrust in front of us...
Why put on a front, why the mindless chatter
That gets us anywhere but where we are,
In this very spot?

Why the why's, Oh Never mind,
Never mind means halt our racing minds!
No need to ponder what is lost,
What has crushed us and destroyed;

Let's start life anew,
Each step in front is a step nonetheless,
So bless it, we are moving somewhere.

Thinking About What Meditation's Meant to Bring...

Call the splendor down from descending spheres,
Sun, eclipse the moon, divide the skies,
Bring forth the rains, stir sand & bones
In deserts dry, a vacancy awaits...

Vacancy, not doom, not blunder nor the torment;
Vacancy, so clear—an empty vessel,
No sands to fill the hourglass, for vanished,
Stripped of substance, no eyes to stare,

No vantage point, just nothing, emptiness...
No thoughts, no sound, no color, no
Day nor night, no space nor time,
No death nor life, no heart nor lung,
No beat nor breath, just the gap,
The pause—word without a syllable—
Outside of Alpha (A) and Omega (O).

Heed the Battle Cry

All things must come to pass,
Whether in this world or the next.
Bitter defeats, ambushes forcing retreats
Strengthen the warrior in the light
Of the sun's discrete degrees;
We shall not concede to the forces of darkness
That blight our progress and bolster misfortune.

Oh, lay up your arms to the Almighty,
From whence comes the seed
Of every good deed, and the tough love
That we, so thirsty in the desert, seek.
My brother seeks You, meek and humble,
Having stumbled, his past a shipwreck,
Terrorist attack and nuclear disaster all combined;
For he's confined without Your love,
Without the tenderness that opens his heart
Like a dove's gentle call.

So he, and I, and you -- heed that battle cry
With the steadfast assurance that Your Word --
The Way, the Truth and the Life -- brings.

Unwinding: Tapping into the Good Ole Divine!

The familiar tunes of a songstress,
Belting out her heart's content.
Old friends, bright and cheerful faces.
The opulence of a bassy hand drum, flanked by melodic piano chops.
Nothing short of tear-invoking, of a Love far deeper than time,
Of a Release pure as the Purest Light.
It's a hymn to the earth, a dedication to the sacred.
It's time to tap out, to tear down the old, cluttered detritus, and peer upon a clean, renewed canvas.
You can paint in tears and pain,
It was meant to be that way.
Beauty releasing pain and sorrow as a flood.
A baby being thrust forth from the womb, into the light of an earthling journey.
The poet is tired.
Life bears down on him.
But it all must go - the inertia, the stress, the resistance.
Let the music as a singing muse draw it out of him.

Prayer to the Great Lover

Glowing, yellow-orange,
The candles are in front of me,
While peaceful ambient music plays in the background.
I am getting into the launching pad.
I am cutting off all distractions.

All is well with my soul,
Despite the worst of my shortcomings.

Breathe...
In through the nose,
Out through the mouth.

Here is what I hear:
You are the Great Lover.
And I don't know how to love.
I want Love:
Not craving,
Nor the double-edged sword of desire,
For this appetite is insatiable,
And grows monstrous in its uncontrollable nature.

You are Pure.
I want to be one with You, Great Spirit.
Help me, Great Spirit,
To wake up early and be one with You.
Help me to find the Faith and Oneness
You desired for me
When You thought of creating me,
Before time immemorial.

Oh, Jesu, oh Great One,
Mother, Father, Oneness - You are!
You desire integrity, wholeness,
You desire my broken piece

For the purpose of healing the human race!

I get it again, Great One!
Strength through weakness!
Surrender to win!
Time-out for the clinching play!

Therefore, I give up on myself.
Therefore, I declare that I trust You again,
And the path You have set before me.
You knew that I would be sitting here,
Listing to Far Eastern meditation music,
A beautiful melody through which You communicate.

You set my mind in motion,
Because I sought You.
You focus my thoughts on Oneness
Through the candle's flame.

The purest
Most holy
Most whole
Most innocent
Most ancient
Most happy
Most compassionate
Most lovely
Most spirited
Most wise
Most of mosts –
The real me.

That is what you pull forth,
What you extract.

Bless You, Great Spirit,
And thank You for sustaining my weary soul.

ON PEOPLE & LIFE

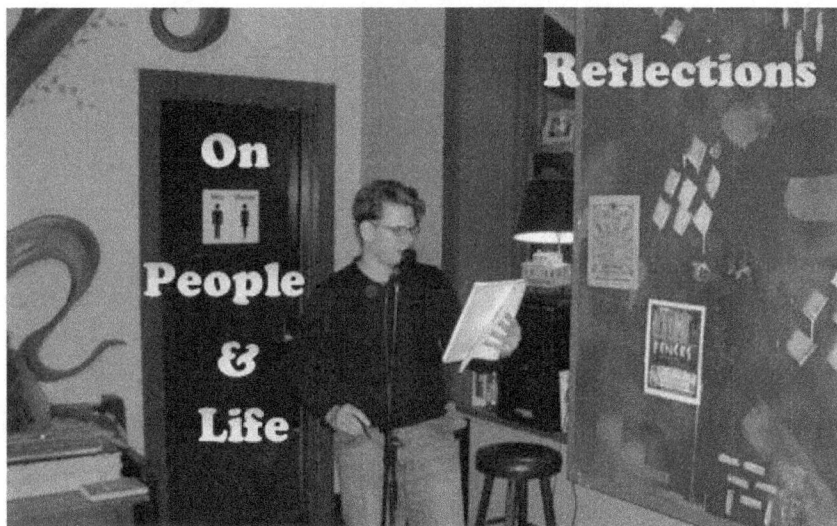

New Mother Teresa

"It's hard to be good in this world,
But you just got to survive."
The new Mother Teresa said this
To a group of bums and derelicts,
And they listened with perked up ears,
While others smirked and laughed
When she told a story of
Riding the bus and listening to
Northeast Philly teens talkin' about
Downing 50 Xannies with bottles of Vodka,
Cursing and swearing, f'n this and f'n that.
She stood up on the bus and zeal poured
Out of her lips that day:
"Do you talk to your mother that way?!"
One of the teens cocked his eyes at her
And said: "My mother doesn't ride the bus."
Talk about asinine. But the new Mother Teresa
Let her values stand, and the whole bus heard her.

Cedar Smoke Fire

Dry cedar, wood smoked fire; open hearth to open heart
To memories of home-cooked bliss.

It's the campfire on an open range.
It dispels the pains of the day's hard luck draw.
A calloused hand empties meager provisions
Into a cast-iron crock pot
As flames flicker
To the grumbling bellies of starving cowboys.

It's Grand-papa adding another log
To the crackling stone fireplace
Where three generations
Absorb stories of bygone days,
Of endless sunsets,
Of young love before they were born,
Of war,
Of peace,
Of the People
(he makes sure not to insult their heritage
By invoking the mockery of their Western monikers)
That loved and venerated the primordial,
Sacred Mother Earth and all of HER family.

The dry cedar, wood smoke eclipses all these settings.
The fire, and its inherent fragrance,
Of the deep treasures of a sacred earth,
Creates life, preserves life, evolves life.

Fire and its essence beckons.

I Can Understand

I can understand how you want to
Run away
Yes, escape
Go and rest your weary bones,
Heart and soul
In a home-cooked café
In a new small town
Where no one knows your name
Or that you've been through hell.
I can understand
In that café
On that stool next to yours
I've lived and breathed
Your escapes
And geographical cures
Your worries and your fears
That took you to this very café counter
On this very stool.

Morning Crickets

The morning crickets are electric.
They rub their legs together in unison,
In harmony, perfect syncopation
As the dew upon the ground swells to fruition.

The morning crickets are sentries
Assigned by the Great Spirit
To perpetuate stasis on the earth's floor. ...
Their vibrations arouse the minutest of life forms
Into action, an intuitive symbiosis
To sustain their corner of the biosphere.
The Morning Crickets help the humans
Meditate to start their week,
Where concerns over money, jobs, relationships,
And the like threaten to destroy their delicate balance.
Breathe in with each rub of their legs,
Breathe out, listening for the pause between their electric rhythms.
Why can't human life be as simple and as peaceful,
As inherently balanced as that of the animal kingdom?

When Joey Ramone Died

I was listening to the Ramones
Feelin' good, shaking my legs and bangin' my head
In good spirits, free thru the music
Like we used to be
When I thought of you
Your laugh
Your smile
God, did we have fun in those years
The music became the "X" of our superconsciousness
Marking the spot of our freedom
And love of fun and life

I wonder how you felt when Joey Ramone died
There was an empty space
In my heart for you on that day
I wish I could have been there for you
All our punk idols have died it seems,
Just like the goth days of dress-up,
Make-up and getting bashed
In the mosh pit by skin heads,
Dyeing our hair and laughing all night long
The Rock Horror Picture Show,
Grease
The Breakfast Club
All the great things we did
Nineteen and out of our minds
But the music saved us

It was listening to the Ramones
Looking at the sky, seeing shooting stars
Those were the days
You were there in a dream last night
We were happy with each other
Like we used to be
And now, I think of you
Your laugh
Your smile
God, did we Rock
And most of all, the music saved us

Gum All Over Your Tux

Synthesizers and lead guitars
Remind me of listening to
80s music at your house,
Blasting your little boom box,
Looking at porn and drooling
Over the women of our
Lust visions and dreams.

Sure, now I know, that
Your dream on this earth
Was limited, no more buxom
Babes to frustrate you or
Tease your natural mind:
For you are now a spirit,
Not confined in a flesh
And blood vessel racked
With pain and diminished
Mental and emotional acumen.

I will write these words,
And they will march on
With me on this journey of life,
In your memory, my late friend
Of backyard baseball, street
And basement hockey, and many
Struggles we've seen each other through.

You were one of the proud ushers
At my wedding; the marriage was a
Disaster and quick to implode,
But you getting gum all over your tux
Was classic, and that moment
Will never die, but rather will be
Played back many times
By many light-hearted souls.

I hope your new journey
Is an exciting one, and that
It will be filled with the
Best dance moves, sports,

And of course, the most
Beautiful women
That we could never had
Laid eyes upon on this earth :)

Underneath Those Unassuming Brown Leaves

In three short days,
It will be the 2nd anniversary of my father's death.
And two years later,
There is still no headstone for his grave.
My grandparents' graves,
Brightly lit by one rectangular headstone
In the mid-afternoon November sun, stand proud.

My dad is buried directly behind them,
Underneath the leaves.
 In the haste of graveyard reconstruction,
Gravel was dumped on the dirt that marked his grave.
Yet, no unkind words have been exchanged
Between the construction crew
And my father's family, including me.

In the hustle and bustle of everyday life
Since his death,
My dad certainly has not been forgotten.
His presence clings to the walls of our house,
Especially the big blue recliner
where he spent so many evenings by the tube,
Eating salted peanuts and drinking straight gin.

An outside observer might think of our family
As being negligent and cold
For still failing to memorialize my father
With a headstone for his grave.
Yet with each and every passing day,
We still can't believe that he's there,
Underneath those unassuming brown leaves,
Left to wither and decay.

EPIPHANIES

The Gift

It's not insane, I'm trying not to go insane.
My thoughts cannot comprehend the liveliness
Of a thousand stars, and blessed and fallen
Upon the earth they are; I wish, I wish upon
A star—words they've said, have been repeated,
Across the great, wide globe. I'm not searching,
I'm not running, I'm not trying to elude myself;
I'm not caught in a trap, I'm not veering off the map—
But what would be nice is a lively chat.

With whom, nobody knows, but the future shows,
In my presence is some sort of compassionate spirit—
Energy of acceptance, a vibe of generosity; oh wow,
The sun looks so cool right now, its enclosure bright;
I'm not lying when I tell you what I'm feeling, there's
Nothing (no feeling) that I'm concealing.
I have to prosper here with my own thoughts,
The truly real part of me—the part that only a few
Can see; they need to see, they need to feel who I am—
Whether the word they're looking for is "sane"
Or something much more catastrophic.

Man, this scene's so much I've seen before,
But only in the realm of feeling; Deja Vu,
But it's totally new, entire to my sense of being.
I'm not trying to spin a web, the old, dirty
Clothing must be shed—I'm a snake, but fresh and new
With the lustre of a newly polished, balding head;
It don't matter, 'cause you want to know why?
Because my mind's already shattered, that's
The reason why it truly doesn't matter.

I'm not lying, but I must reassure you,
As well as myself—that this conversation
Could not exist without compliance, patience,
Understanding, inspiration, dynamite expression—
All encompassed within the gift. The gift which
All of us possess, I must confess, deny it if you will.

I'll tell you, though, the gift could not exist,

Nor persist, If I went on a bender and ended up
In a cloud of inebriation; I'm not apologizing
For anything nor to anyone, just restating who I am,
And what I stand for. Focus, of the mind, the spirit,
Beyond the flesh—like a flash in a pan my spirit winds
Far around, never knowing when it will hit the ground.
My wrist's so sore, Goddamn it now! I take that back,
I love You God, and I know that You love me—
You're simply telling me that it's time to stop.

Maori Spirit Ascension

There is something special at this moment,
When one learns what happens when
A Maori Spirit ascends from this earth,
Through the sacred tree on the cliffs
By the waters of the Tasman Sea.
The fierce winds stop for a second,
All the villagers hold their breath at once—
And the spirit ascends, and as it does,
The winds pick up, roar fiercely like battle horns,
And the Maori chant in tones and harmonies
Of which Westerners could only dream.

Answer to My Question of What Is Heaven

Pristine night, not a speck of cloud
In the clear blue dome of the sky;
Friends talking late into the evening,
Listening to the voice of the waterfall,
New adventures in the wild green yonder
Now conceiving.

If someone asked you what made heaven in you,
What would you say?

In other words, what makes you
High with ecstatic joy?

The woods, talks with friends by a bonfire
Or a rushing stream, union with the energy
Of the Bear Spirit is my answer to this question.

Now, what is yours?

Microcosms

These souls are the ones I miss.
Like chlorophyll to spring leaves
They are my chemistry.

We are children trying to grow up
In a world dominated by abusive, adult egos.
Let's not lose our essence.
Let's not dry up like potted plants
That sit neglected, baking in the sun,
Without a drop of water.

Your humor is me.
Your beauty, your words
Are my mental orgasm.

Souls like this are the ones I wander from,
Like a hermit from society,
Like a vampire from the sunlight.

We are all microcosms,
Teeming with our freedoms,
Which we cannot express
In the clinical, cubicle world.

Leaf through an Open Window

A sigh, a breath, a gust of wind
Blowing a leaf through an open window.
Motion, change, transformation,
Transmutation, ever-evolving shapes,
Puzzle pieces being refitted,
New totems on new trees
Mirroring the breeze
That never blows the same way twice.

Intersecting Moments

We're so alive, each day,
But fail to see,
All the intersecting moments
That breathe the breaths
that set us free.
Insidious thoughts of defeat
Convince us that the sky is black
Instead of blue and
That we are our own worst enemies.
Life is too short to be stuck,
Forlorn, in chains that bind.
Let us beckon to the call
So we can free our minds.
God's inmost desires for our souls
Is wholeness,
In every parcel, in every part.
This is the challenge to me, to you:
Now are you ready to start?

It's Hard to Communicate (All These Miracles)

"It's hard to communicate all these miracles…"
The last words my dad spoke
On this planet before he passed on.
They are now etched on his gravestone.

It's over ten years later
And now I finally know what he means.
There are more than a few –
They are flowing in abundance,
Like a river.

I have become the person
I always wanted to be.
I have become filled with the Spirit,
And God has led me to my dreams.

I am fulfilled.
I love other people and want to see them
Also reach and live their dreams.
I understand and now experience
Love to be beyond my wildest imaginings –
On every level.

These are miracles.
Angels have protected me
Along the way, and continue to do so.

The relationships
That have come into my life
Are evidence of these miracles
My dad spoke of,
While he was without a doubt
Fully in the flow
Of God's light, His Holy Spirit.

My gratitude is beyond words,
But I attempt them anyway.
I am grateful, and yes:
"It's hard to communicate…
All these miracles."

LOST SOULS

Baby, Leave Me Be

Now you see me,
There you go…
In the neon twilight
Your scarlet aura overshadows mine,
Sends the lightning, icy tumult,
Through my placid face…

That such was the case
When you were there to blame—
I apologize—it's nothing but
A coward's spiteful lie—

Go away, disappear into the wind,
Let me be—may your tender
Copulation find another man—
Baby leave me be—I'm
Drowning, shipwrecked out at sea—
Not your trouble, not your time…

Sometimes I'm dying—but I'd never
Tell you that—I shouldn't have to—
If you were to look, for a moment,
Not too deep—You would
See the troubled times.

Tragedy of a Fateful Malady

Headed for the end—
Lightly tap my feet a little,
Before too long, I descend…
And reach high above the clouds,
One with the sun, and as it recedes
And the day goes down so do I—
To become one with my eternal, blessed mother,
The night's all reigning goddess—
And I know my time has come.

Obituary Page

Why am I such a fucking junkie
For a love that cannot be fulfilled?
Why do I write this bullshit down,
Thinking it's the ticket out,
Out of this miserable existence I have lived?

Will someone find my letters buried far beneath
After they read about my tragic death upon the obituary page?
All I need is someone to listen to my plea,
My microscopic quest for somber tenderness—

Why can't the world explode, for everyone would see—
The truth, I hope, the real nature of the beast!!
We, the race of beasts, know nothing, really nothing…
Blind with death we walk around, in circles never-ending…

Perhaps by now you can see one thing is clear
Hope my dismal, ruthless words are ringing in your ears:
This emptiness, this loneliness, this bitterness—
All because I am such a fucking junkie
For a love that cannot be fulfilled.

The Lies That Lay Between Us

What secrets do you spin
Within the lines of text
That weave the story of your life?
Are you a crying child on the inside,
Not knowing the travesties that deceive,
What in this clockwork world is there to believe?

From the outside looking in,
You soul is weighed in lead,
Knowing all the times of broken dreams
And how deeply wounded you have bled.

The religion could not help you
Through your torrential ways,
No one that you met could
Assuage the wound of yesterday.

What about the broken hearts
That laid you dormant for so long?
Could you cut your way against
The icy wind that beat you down?

Subtle, well-hidden was your game,
A creature that no one could tame,
A child of starlit nights, lamenting
Silent sorrow into astral flight.

Enigma in a Mask

We were high school losers,
Dead, without a brain.

Mindless of the virgin birth,
Intent on getting laid.

But I was the only one,
To walk the plank, it seems.

So I hopped the ship
In hot pursuit of delusory dreams.

Of course I had a mistress,
A mother queen to some.

Crowning her, I staked my claim,
And yelled that I had won.

I was the secret winner,
True, and with an aim.

Heartful of the thrills of sex,
I fucked until I came.

Just a king for one grand day,
The canvas soon came down.

I couldn't talk about my queen
Lest I breed ungodly frowns.

No such thing as virgin birth,
No such way as veiled and pure.

The gods they had me trapped,
My classmates never asked.

So I went from high school loser
To that enigma in a mask.

Live a Death like This

Idleness is the devil's workshop,
So you must work, work, work
And keeping working to make
The bad dreams go away
So the blue skies can shine.

Work means getting up every day,
Wanting to live, even though each
Joint, fiber and muscle in your body
Aches for rest it will never get,
Most likely, till retirement or an early death.

And it is idleness, the devil's workshop
(Or "playground" for you idiomatic conservatives)
That causes another type of early death—
Steeped in absolute hopelessness
In front of the tube, sleeping all day,
Or drugged and drunk out of your mind,
Of no use to society and its inhabitants.
Do you want to live a death like this?

Faces in the Fire

Staring at the fire's warm embers,
I'm reminded of being a kid again,
Seeing faces where the dark ashes
Meet that fiery glow.
Some of the faces are friendly,
Some are scary, some constant throughout the night.
And the faces reflected the gazes
Of the people around me,
Sitting about the fire, listening to stories
As marshmallows were nuked and slapped
Onto pieces of milk chocolate and gram crackers.
To this day, the faces have never changed,
Though the people sitting around the fire with me
Have grown older, wiser,
And filled with more joy and pain
In life's ascending and descending experiences
Through all types of terrain.

I Am a Sinner

I am a sinner.
From the very bowels
Of my lowest low I am a sinner.
My sickness is shame, faceless,
Formless, set on only pleasing itself
And objectifying and devaluating
God's creations of beauty and tranquility.
I know I have done wrong.
Yet I bear the guilt of my loneliness
And misshapen identity, mistaken,
Misguided sexuality, for I am truly lost.
I am a sinner. Each time I'm
On the verge of the heavenly path,
It seems, I slip and fall from grace
And dwell in hell, in disfiguredness,
Disrobed for unfaithfulness to seduce
My inmost innocence...
And take U along for the ride.
I am a sinner.
I wallow in bogs
And the filthiest cesspools of existence,
And wonder how I got there.
I want to ask your forgiveness
For the path I tread in my dark hours,
But fear you'll never want to know
Where it is that I have tread,
And what fires and floods I have scorched
And deluged this land of spirits walking
In flesh bodies in society.
For I am terminally unique,
And lest you forget this, I will die this way.
I am a sinner.

KINGDOM'S REJECTS

From Whence Dost Thou Spring?

The doors to perception have beckoned Your calling;
The ways through the haze in the realm of the mind
Are perceived, the small beam of light directly enthralling;
The purpose, the rhyme, the unknown now defined.

What about the villains, the victims of the darkness
Who stand, ball and chain, fettered, confined?
Do they know of warmth, resilience from starkness?
Those fettered are freed, released from their crimes.

The legion of darkness had swallowed them whole,
When rock bottom and broken they heard Your voice.
Out of their caves they proceeded, tarnished in soul,
And collapsed to their knees of their own choice.

"Where art Thou, from whence dost thou spring?
I'm dying and hopeless, I know I have sinned!
Please prove You exist, and with praises I'll sing.
I'm not a believer, but please lead me within!"

It was at this moment frozen in time
That the wretch conceded Yours was the light;
That the light of the dayspring surely did shine,
And no matter how lost, Your way he could find.

Liquefied By Your Light

I am bowing my head, closing my eyes,
And saying a prayer, because,
Behind this invisible wall between me and You,
I know that You are there.

I know that You are there
Despite all the seeming evidence
To the contrary in how I've lived my life,
In all the dark places I've led my mind.

In all the dark places I've led my mind,
I know that even if I didn't feel it in my heart,
You were with me every step.

You were with me every step,
Every breath, sluggish as it may have been.
So when I am afraid or sense
That soon my fragile mind will break,
I cry out like that man lost in the wilderness.

I cry out like that man lost in the wilderness,
And like the people lost in darkness
Who have seen Your light, I am filled instantly,
An injection of serum from the Holy of Holies,
And my soul is restored.

And my soul is restored,
Again in each instance of temptation,
Loss and anguish that I give to You.
As I look outside, on the cold, rainy pavement,
The white painted arrow points forward,
Showing me the path You have designated for me.

Showing me the path You have designated for me,
I follow. And with each step I swallow, my pride
And everything that has befallen me and my elders,
And move down this path, till my rusty limbs come alive,
Liquefied by Your Light and the belief in action
I chose on the verge of giving up.

His LML (Labors, Mercy, Love)

I ran away from the pain,
But I'm left here today,
Hurting and sighing
As the rain cascades;
I feel a break with the world around me.

For I know on the other side of this cloud
Is a shout that rings aloud,
A triumphant light
That leads souls from the darkness,
As the voice of the Lord
Within me hearkens.

Yeah, it hearkens,
And dispels the hardships,
Sets the misfits on a straight path,
Where they are no longer
Subject to His wrath, but rather,
His Labors and His Mercy and His Love.

Be Our Escape

Helpless as a baby in the cradle,
You feel warm arms embrace you.
Warm arms penetrate like
A bubble bath upon frigid skin
In the cold of winter.

Your breath - exhalations
In gasps and stitches, asynchronous,
Like palpitations of an off-beat heart.
Nerves and muscles - tight -
Cling against your battle-wearied bones.

You are at the end of the rope,
The last station;
The final square foot of asphalt
On a dead-end street:
A dead-end street they call DEFEAT.

DEFEAT:
Not just losing, but lost, a loser;
DEFEAT:
Not just an unwinding thread,
But unwound:

Oh, how on sunny days and hot nights
Long past you walked so proud!
Alas, they are no more;
Your triumphs are like once ample
Bank accounts now bankrupt, gone.

Hopeless -
In a tunnel, not seeing a speck of light.
You want to believe,
But believing surely means to see,
Perceive, and feel:

Instead, you are despairing,
And raging, pining, reviling:
All the things and articles of happiness
You see wrought in the lives around you,

In the world at large.

Sinking -
Your ship is a sinking boat,
But lest you forget -
You have a life vest,
And an island of safety does exist -
Though not within the purview
Of your ailing human eyes.

That life vest, that island, that ray of light -
Is faith in your Savior
When all hope is gone,
All safety stripped away,
When you're defeated,
And there's nowhere left to go:

Fall at the throne of Grace,
Reach for His ankles, a timeless embrace;
Tell Him you need Him,
Tell Him you need to hear from Him -
Tell Him, right now,
That you just want His love,
Just need Him near.
Ask Him to lift you,
Ask Him to heal you,
Ask Him to thaw your frozen heart
And give You a new start
In a life marred by train wrecks,
And wounds caused by Satan.

"I pray Thee, Father,
And my Lord, Jesus Christ,
To take this burden from me.
Help me, your lost and aching child,
To find my way back home;
Help me, Father, be my shelter,
Be my one and all,
From everlasting to everlasting;
Be with me, for I'm afraid,
I'm ashamed, I'm depraved,
There's a smoking mountain

Of rubble left in my wake!
Help me, Lord Jesus, be my escape."

Be our escape, Lord -
For only You can deliver our souls
From the devil's hoof
And unimpale us
From the world's spears and hooks.

Clay / the Potter

"But now, O LORD,
You are our father;
We are the clay, and You our potter.
And we all are the work of Your hand."
 - Isaiah 64:8

Please, I beg,
Take and mold
This twisted shape,
This lumpen meld
Of flesh and bone.

Break me down,
Refine me,
Try my impurity,
And with impunity
Flatten me,
Make me malleable.

Fire up Your kiln,
Prepare the fire
To burn away my dross.

Oh, powerful hands,
My Lord, form a chalice,
Worthy to hold Your Living Waters.

All I have to offer now
Is this wretched soul,
Darker than the blackest coal.

Please make me whole:
Smash my delusions,
Decimate my idols,
Anodize my pain, my agony.

Make me selfless,
Able to bear this cross
And carry Your precious gospel
To the sick and suffering.

Recreate this cup,
Weathered as it may be.
Help me Lord, my Potter,
Knead Your life in me. Amen.

Feasting: My Portion

"The Lord is my portion1, says my soul;
Therefore will I hope in Him.
The Lord is good to them that wait for Him,
To the soul that seeks Him.
It is good that a man should
Both hope and wait quietly
For the salvation of the Lord."

- Lamentations 3: 24-26

What banquet do you feast at?
And, who are your dinner guests?
No, the question should really be,
"Where do you get your nourishment?"

Is your portion media clips
Of sultry creeds,
Or works of money, greed?
Or do you devour music profane
To empower your soul
In this final hour?

Your portion is what you consume –
What you eat and drink in
Through your eyes, ears, nose, mouth,
And then digest, and become one with.

What will it take
To make the King your portion?
Do you devour His Word
And the promise of salvation
Like there's no other meal on the menu?

Sometimes, we are impatient
And consume what feels good
To our flesh –
Making our "portion" the idols of this world.

---

[1] Food, or "Filling"

Let the Lord be your portion.
Let Him do His work in you.
Feed on Him, drink Him in.
Wait for Him,
And don't hesitate to believe.

Kingdom's Rejects

"There will be no more sorrow,
No crying, no dying, no pain;
For the One who so loves us,
Will lift all our troubles away."

All across a dim-lit room are kindred souls,
Stung, having succumbed to the dispersion
Of poisons disguised as anodynes,
Shortcut to a bliss counterfeit;
We are old, young, druggies, drunkies,
Street preachers, dons, pimps, hoes,
Pervs, cornerboys –
All broken by to smithereens by life,
A life in which we bought the lie
And on our pride tried to ride the tide
To topple castles only to be locked inside
Spiritual prisons without keys:

But now, we are freed, we are freed,
By a Light that shined for the sick to see,
So we all crawled to Him and on bended knees
Asked Him our all and everything to be:

And we heard it:

"There will be no more sorrow,
No crying, no dying, no pain;
For the One who so loves us,
Will lift all our troubles away."

So in this darkened tunnel we now see,
Perceive a light – and give up the fight,
The fight of fright and the blight
Of wreckage we've left behind.
We are but diamonds inside cavernous mines,
Holy Spirit containers waiting to be filled,
To seek a thrill beyond all thrills,
To leave behind all of the madness,
All of the sadness, yeah,
To leave it all once and for all.

So we listened to the words of the Word – Word! –
And something inside began to stir –
Tears of joy eclipsed our pain,
We saw the Savior's light inside our brains,
And the song of hope to help us cope:

"There will be no more sorrow,
No crying, no dying, no pain;
For the One who so loves us,
Will lift all our sorrows away."

But then the battle, it was ON:
Parents and sisters and neighbors
Who'd done so well by their good alms,
Buying stained glass windows for their churches,
Being as pious and neatly-dressed as
Righteous could be,
"Jesus? Now your tripping on Jesus?"
You're nothin' but a dope fiend, an irreligious twit,
And now you say, you say, "Jesus is it?"

Yes, we do – it's all we got to hang onto,
We're nothin' but a bunch of freaks,
Misfits burnt out by the need for love,
The need for more, and we're left devoid,
With nothing – when He came to us.
We are broken, we are crippled,
We are blinded, we are without recourse,
And in need of the ultimate Resource:
Hope of a better life,
Where there is no suffering or strife,
In the arms of our Daddy up above,
Being transformed by His love.

For in Heaven:

"There will be no more sorrow,
No crying, no dying, no pain;
For the One who so loves us,
Will lift all our troubles away."

We are the druggies, drunkies, bums, pimps,
Hoes, pervs and rejects for the Lord;
For He calls not the righteous,
But sinners to repentance.
He calls us because this hell on earth
Has been our sentence,
Where we caught and tore our souls
On proverbial razor wire fences,
To be left for dead –
Both physically and spiritually
In need of bread – and water,
The elixir of life, so we could survive
And be revived – revived by His Living Water,
That our love for Him would grow much hotter.

"There will be no more sorrow,
No crying, no dying, no pain;
For the One who so loves us,
Will lift all our troubles away."

We are fodder, we are refuse,
We are crack-pot broken pots
In need of a Potter – to pick us up,
Shards of lifeless clay, to be meld
Into His ways, to quit the endless maze
Of this world's paths of craze.
We don't stand, we barely walk,
We limp through life,
For every day we fight,
Fight to stay alive in the Spirit of God
So our great Enemy won't run us roughshod
And destroy us
To the last atomic fissure of our beings.

We pray because we don't have a prayer.
We gather, we pray, we listen to His Word
And keep coming back;
Yeah, we keep coming back,
Because He loves us,
Yes, He loves us,
And sings so sweetly, sings our souls to sleep,
To peaceful sleep:

"There will be no more sorrow,
No crying, no dying, no pain;
For the One who so loves us,
Will lift all our troubles away."

"There will be no more sorrow,
No crying, no dying, no pain;
For the One who so loves us,
Will lift all our troubles away."

ABOUT THE AUTHOR

Nils Ljungberg (pronounced "young-berg") Odhner was born on July 2, 1976 in Meadowbrook, Pennsylvania.

Nils found his calling in 1995 when he picked up a pen and wrote his first poem. Since then, he has composed thousands of poems, several short stories, and one full-length novel.

His poems and short stories have appeared in The Philadelphia Tribune, The Theta Alpha Journal, and the Philadelphia Online Arts Journal (HINGE). Nils graduated with a B.A in English and Creative Writing from Bryn Athyn College in 2000.

www.ingramcontent.com/pod-product-compliance
Lightning Source LLC
Chambersburg PA
CBHW032141040426
42449CB00005B/346